INSPIRATIONAL LIVES

LEWIS HAMILTON

FORMULA ONE CHAMPION

Clive Gifford

WAYLAND

First published in 2011 by Wayland

Copyright © Wayland 2011

Wayland
338 Euston Road
London NW1 3BH

Wayland Australia
Level 17/207 Kent Street
Sydney, NSW 2000

Editor: Nicola Edwards
Designer: Paul Cherrill

British Library cataloguing in
Publication Data:
Gifford, Clive.
Lewis Hamilton: Formula One champion.
-- (Inspirational lives)
  1. Hamilton, Lewis, 1985- --Juvenile
  literature.
  2. Automobile racing drivers--Great
  Britain--Biography--Juvenile literature.
I. Title II. Series
796.7'2'092-dc22

ISBN: 978 0 7502 6481 5

Printed in China

Wayland is a division of Hachette
Children's Books, an Hachette UK
company.

www.hachette.co.uk

Picture acknowledgements: The author
and publisher would like to thank the
following for allowing their pictures to
be reproduced in this publication: Cover,
pp4, 5, 6 Getty Images, p7 Rui Vieira/
PA Wire; pp8-9 Sutton/Sutton/Press
Association Images; pp10-11 Getty Images;
p12 Getty Images; p13 A3416 Carmen
Jaspersen/DPA/Press Association Images;
p14 NULL/Sutton/Press Association
Images; p15 HERMANN J. KNIPPERTZ/
AP/Press Association Images; pp16-17
Sutton/Sutton/Press Association Images;
p18 Getty Images; p19 NULL/Sutton/
Press Association Images; p20 MICHAEL
SOHN/AP/Press Association Images; p21
Oliver Multhaup/AP/Press Association
Images; p22 Victor R. Caivano/AP/Press
Association Images; p23 Graham Hughes/
The Canadian Press/Press Association
Images; p24 Oliver Multhaup/AP/Press
Association Images; p25 Rui Vieira/
PA Archive/Press Association Images;
p26 Getty Images; p27 David Davies/
PA Archive/Press Association Images;
p28 Anthony Devlin/PA Archive/Press
Association Images; p29 Sutton/PA
Photos/Sutton/Press Association Images

Contents

World Champion!

November 2nd 2008. The last race of the Formula One World Championship. All eyes were on Britain's exciting young driver, Lewis Hamilton. He needed to finish in fifth place or better to defeat Ferrari's Felipe Massa and be crowned World Champion. It was only his second season in Formula One – the fastest and most demanding form of motor racing.

TOP TIP

In his **autobiography**, *My Story*, published in 2007, Lewis wrote that he always tries to stay positive even when he is losing a race or facing a problem. He says that every new day offers new opportunities to learn and improve.

The race was held on the Interlagos circuit in Brazil. The track was bumpy in places but fast, with cars on the Reta Oposa straight reaching top speeds of 320km/h. Lewis was in fifth place during the race when it started raining, making the track wet and slippery. He found that his tyres weren't getting as much grip as some of his rivals'. With just two laps to go, he was overtaken by Sebastian Vettel. Lewis slipped down to sixth place. It seemed his hopes of winning the championship were over.

Lewis moves into fifth place ahead of Timo Glock and Jarno Trulli in the final race of the 2008 season.

Felipe Massa crossed the finish line to win the race and, it appeared, the whole Drivers' World Championship. His Ferrari team started celebrating in the **pit lane**. However, just 35 seconds behind Massa, amazing drama was unfolding.

On the very last corner of the 71st and last lap of the track Lewis went for broke. He swooped past Timo Glock to regain fifth place moments before crossing the line. His McLaren team-mates were overjoyed. Their young driver was World Champion.

Lewis became not only Britain's ninth Formula One World Champion since the competition began in 1950 but also the first black driver from any country to win the championship. That's not all. At the age of just 23, he was the youngest to be crowned World Champion. It was an extraordinary achievement.

Lewis celebrates being world champion with his half-brother Nicholas, his father Anthony, his stepmother Linda and his girlfriend Nicole Scherzinger from the girl group the Pussycat Dolls.

INSPIRATION

"Dad is my biggest supporter and a fantastic father without whom I may not have even discovered I had any talent for racing." – Lewis Hamilton.

Growing up

Lewis Carl Davidson Hamilton was born on January 7th 1985 and grew up in a council house in Shepsall, Stevenage, north of London. When he was two years old, his mother, Carmen and father, Anthony split up. His parents stayed in touch and Lewis saw his father at weekends. Both his Mum and Dad remained strong, positive influences on the young Lewis.

Anthony's father, Davidson Hamilton, **emigrated** from the Caribbean island of Grenada to Britain in 1955 to work on the London Underground. Anthony also worked in public transport, for British Rail. He started out as an administration clerk but worked his way up to computer manager.

WOW!

Lewis played football in the same school team as Aston Villa and England football star, Ashley Young.

Lewis is hugged by both his mother, Carmen (right) and stepmother, Linda after winning the 2008 Chinese Grand Prix.

Lewis went to Peartree Junior School, a five-minute walk from his home. His teachers remember him as a happy pupil who worked hard. When Lewis was bullied in the playground, he decided to gain confidence by learning a martial art for self defence. Together with his father he enrolled at Stevenage Karate Club and threw himself in to learning the sport. Lewis did so well that he was awarded a grade just below black belt. In 2009, by then a Formula One World Champion, Lewis was a special guest at the karate club's 30th anniversary dinner.

At school Lewis enjoyed playing a wide range of sports. He threw the javelin and ran the 800m in athletics. He also made the school basketball and cricket teams. His best school sport, though, was football, even though Lewis wrote in his autobiography that he always seemed to work twice as hard but only get half the performance of some of his team-mates. He was destined for success in a completely different sport.

Lewis and Anthony smile for the cameras the day after Lewis had become the youngest ever Formula One world champion.

TOP TIP

Martial arts such as karate, judo and taekwondo are activities you can learn out of school that can be great fun and give you extra self-confidence.

Starting karting

Lewis first drove a go-kart when he was on holiday on the Spanish island of Ibiza. The vehicle was a tiny electric go-kart for small children and it didn't go very fast, but he loved driving it. Lewis quickly became car mad, watching Grand Prix races on TV with his dad. For his fifth birthday, Lewis received a battery-powered remote controlled car. He played with it so much that his father bought him a bigger, faster model a few months later.

Lewis and Anthony joined a local model car racing club in Stevenage. Out of the 50 or so members, Lewis was one of the only children, but it didn't stop him winning races against adults.

WOW!

Lewis was just six years old when he appeared on TV demonstrating his skills at racing remote control cars on the children's programme Blue Peter.

Success comes early: Lewis poses with a winner's trophy and a garland of flowers. His family home quickly filled with karting trophies.

After a year of racing model cars, Lewis got the chance to drive a real go-kart at the Rye House track close to his home. He was just seven but amazed his father with his natural racing skills. Even on his first drive, he seemed to know instinctively how to turn well into corners, when to go faster and when to slow down.

Lewis' karting career took him all over Britain and Europe where he raced on indoor and outdoor tracks.

Anthony decided to support his son and spent more than a whole month's wages on a battered old go-kart which he rebuilt over many evenings in his shed. Lewis was thrilled when he was presented with the kart and a red crash helmet on Christmas Day.

As soon as he was eight years old, Lewis was able to race at Rye House in the Cadet Class. This is the first level of motor racing in Britain for 8- to 12-year-olds. Lewis was a keen competitor straight away, challenging for the lead in races against drivers who had two or three years of experience. He won his first Cadet race at Rye House by the end of January 1993. Many more would follow.

INSPIRATION

Lewis' father gave him constant encouragement during the early days of karting. He also urged Lewis to push himself harder and to learn from other more experienced racers.

Moving home

Lewis' life changed when he was ten. His mother and her new partner were moving to London. Everyone decided that Lewis would stay in Stevenage where he was happy at school and enjoying his kart racing. He moved in with his father, Anthony and his new stepmother, Linda.

Lewis and Linda got on extremely well from the start. In many interviews, Lewis calls Linda the best stepmother in the world and believes he would not have succeeded without the huge amount of love and support he received from her as well as from his mum and dad.

Lewis now had a half-brother, Nicholas. As a toddler, Nicholas was found to have cerebral palsy. People with cerebral palsy suffer a wide range of difficulties, such as finding it hard to walk or stand still as well as struggling to speak. Nicholas was in and out of hospital for operations yet always remained a strong, cheerful child.

WOW!

Lewis and Nicholas are fond of playing car racing games on computer consoles. Lewis tends to win but Nicholas is usually only a second behind.

Lewis pushes Nicholas in his wheelchair three days before the 2007 Belgian Grand Prix. Nicholas often watches Lewis' races and knows a lot about Formula One.

Lewis and Nicholas became incredibly close as children, playing computer games, golf and other sports together despite Nicholas' difficulties. Lewis was constantly impressed by his brother's determination to overcome his disabilities.

In his autobiography, Lewis wrote: "I often try to imagine myself in Nic's position. I do not think I would be anywhere near as strong as him. There's just so much to admire in him...so Nic is my inspiration and that helps me a lot."

Lewis, with his brother, father and stepmother, meet Nelson Mandela before a dinner to celebrate the great statesman's 90th birthday. Lewis has said of the meeting that 'it was like walking in to see the king. To be in front of God.'

INSPIRATION

According to Lewis, Nicholas is, "a great person, always positive." He says, "I have learned so much from him - for example, that one can solve any problem. If things don't go well, I think of him."

Making sacrifices

Once Lewis started winning karting races he found it hard to stop. His family went with him all over the country, his dad's Vauxhall Cavalier towing Lewis' go-kart behind it in beaten up trailer. In 1995, Lewis entered the British Cadet Kart Championship and won the entire competition. His future in racing was bright – but the costs were mounting up.

Ten-year-old Lewis sits and waits for the fog to lift before racing at a karting track in Northampton in 1995.

Competitive karting is an expensive business. A single weekend in racing could mean having to spend over £300 just on fuel and tyres alone. Then there was the expense of travelling to races and practice sessions, as well as race entry fees. Major parts for the kart could cost thousands of pounds. Anthony showed enormous dedication by taking on extra jobs including putting up estate agents' 'For Sale' signs for £15 per sign. He spent all his spare time tinkering with Lewis's kart or dreaming up new ways of raising funds for racing.

WOW!

Lewis has raced in a yellow coloured helmet since before he was a teenager. His father chose the colour so that he could spot Lewis racing even on the far side of a track.

Luckily for the Hamiltons the karting community in Britain is very friendly. Others recognised Lewis' ability and helped the family out with parts and equipment. Among those who helped were Martin Hines, owner of the Zipkart company, and John Button, father of Jenson who would become Formula One World Champion a year after Lewis.

Anthony Hamilton discusses business with Formula One boss Bernie Ecclestone. Anthony managed Lewis' career for over 15 years.

When Anthony was refused extra leave from work to support Lewis, he left his job with British Rail and took on several part-time jobs, including running his own business, to give him the money and the time to help build Lewis's racing career. Lewis had to make sacrifices too, as all his spare time was taken up by racing or travelling to races and catching up on his school homework. As the race wins continued to mount, it all seemed worth it.

INSPIRATION

For Lewis to succeed, his father believed that Lewis had to work really hard and be honest about any problems he faced. The pair would talk through issues all the time.

Joining McLaren

Ten-year-old Lewis, British Formula Cadet Karting Champion, entered the luxurious Grosvenor Park Hotel in London in December 1995 wearing a shiny green suit that was a little too big for him. He had borrowed it from a karting friend as his family couldn't afford to buy their growing son a brand new outfit.

Lewis and his dad were very excited. They were attending the AutoSport Awards and the room was full of the world's most famous motorsports stars. Lewis rushed round the tables collecting autographs of F1 drivers such as Damon Hill and rally racing stars including Colin McRae and Richard Burns. Anthony had made him a special autograph book especially for the event.

Guest of honour at the awards show was Ron Dennis, the powerful boss of the McLaren Formula One team. Lewis walked up to him and, although terribly nervous, looked him straight in the eye. "Hello, I'm Lewis Hamilton," he said. "One day I'd like to be a racing driver and I'd like to race for McLaren."

*Lewis stands with Ron Dennis at the Belgian Grand Prix in 1997. Dennis would be Lewis' **mentor** and guide into the world of adult motorsport.*

Lewis and Dennis talked for a while before Dennis signed his autograph and wrote, "Call me in nine years." Lewis went back to karting and winning races but he had left a positive impression on Dennis who, years later, told reporters, "Unlike so many people, he looked me square in the face and informed me where he was going in his life. Without breaking eye contact, he told me how he was going to go about his career. It impressed the hell out of me."

Lewis didn't have to wait nine years. Just three years after Ron Dennis had written in his autograph book, Lewis was signed to the McLaren Mercedes Young Driver Support Programme. This would help fund his racing. He was just thirteen and the youngest racer connected to any Formula One team.

WOW!

Brothers Colin and Alistair McRae were world-leading rally drivers in 1995. Lewis recalls in his autobiography how, at the AutoSport show, they both chanted his name over and over again, making him laugh.

Lewis guides his kart into a turn at the 2001 CIK-*FIA* World Karting Championship at Kerpen in Germany. Lewis finished seventh behind Nico Rosberg and racing legend, Michael Schumacher.

HONOURS BOARD

Major Karting Honours:

1995 *British Cadet Kart Champion*
1997 *Super 1 National Formula Yamaha Champion*
2000 *European Formula A Champion*
2000 *World Cup Formula A Champion*

Success and setbacks

In the winter of 2001, Lewis made the big jump from driving karts to full-sized racing cars. At the same time, he began studying for his A Levels at a sixth-form college in Cambridge. In the summer holidays, at Anthony's insistence, Lewis found work as a **valet** cleaning cars. Lewis threw himself into the job determined to be the best car valet at the showroom.

TOP TIP

Whatever the job or task, even if it is a part-time job you will only have for a short time, Lewis believes it is important to get to know the other workers and to do your best. That way you can take pride in your work and enjoy it.

The move from karting to cars was bigger than Lewis had imagined. He was employed by Manor Motorsports to race Formula Renault cars. These are single-seater vehicles which look like smaller, less powerful versions of Formula One cars. But they are still real speed machines, capable of accelerating from 0 to 160km/h in under five seconds.

Lewis holds the trophy for winning the 2003 British Formula Renault Championship.

Lewis did well in **qualifying** and started in fifth place on the **grid** in his first British Formula Renault series race. Yet, as the race began, many rival drivers overtook him. Struggling in his first seasons in Formula Renault, he considered quitting for the only time in his racing career. But with the support of his father and the Manor Motorsport team, he persevered.

In 2003, something clicked in Lewis' driving and he had a stunning season. He won 10 of the 15 British Formula Renault races and became champion with two races to spare. He had more to learn when he moved up to Formula Three (F3) the following year. Lewis entered a tough European competition called the F3 Euroseries and finished fifth in 2004. In 2005, he was utterly dominant, winning 15 of the 20 races to be crowned Euroseries Champion.

WOW!

On his very first test drive at the Mallory Park racetrack in Leicestershire, Lewis crashed his Formula Renault car on the third lap. It didn't stop him taking the car straight back onto the track just hours later once it had been rebuilt.

In his bright yellow helmet Lewis races his Manor Motorsport Formula Three car at the Magny-Cours track in France.

Life In GP2

After his final successful year in Formula Three, Lewis made the daunting but exciting step up to **GP2**. This is the major motor racing competition just one level below Formula One. GP2 is packed with exciting, talented young drivers all competing for a rare chance to race in F1.

GP2 cars can reach top speeds of more than 300km/h. All feature the same Renault engines and body frames built by the Dallara racing car company. Driving the same cars as each other gives racers more of an equal chance to shine. The 2006 season featured eleven different racetracks with two races held at each track. Lewis was up against talented young racers such as Timo Glock and Nelson Piquet Jr. Yet, in his very first GP2 feature race, he crossed the line in second place.

Lewis stands on top of his GP2 car after winning his home race at Silverstone in England. Lewis would finish the season 12 points clear of Nelson Piquet Jr. in second place.

At the second race weekend in San Marino, his inexperience led to a setback. He was disqualified from a race for driving in front of a **safety car**. But on the third weekend, he won both his races at Germany's Nurburgring track.

Lewis continued to score points, finishing well in racing all year, winning in front of British fans at Silverstone and building his high speed racing experience throughout the season. At the very last race weekend at the famous Monza track in Italy, he won the GP2 championship.

Over in Formula One, excitement mounted towards the end of the season as many drivers changed teams. At McLaren, both drivers left. Kimi Räikkönen moved to Ferrari and Juan Pablo Montoya left F1 for **NASCAR**. McLaren announced world champion Fernando Alonso as one of their new drivers, but who would be the other?

Lewis hardly dared to dream. After all he was so young. But Ron Dennis broke the news to Lewis and Anthony at the end of September, 2006. Lewis would be racing in F1 the following season.

WOW!

In a GP2 race in Istanbul, Lewis spun his car and fell back to 18th place right at the back of the field. He recovered to take second place on the very last lap of the race.

HONOURS BOARD

In one GP2 season, Lewis notched up an impressive record:

Five wins
Seven second places
Two third places
Six fastest laps

Lewis talks to motor racing legend, Sir Stirling Moss during his successful GP2 season. Moss described Lewis as "The best thing to happen to Formula One in my time".

Welcome to F1

Formula One is the most technical of all motorsports. Tens of millions of pounds are spent on developing an F1 car which can accelerate from 0 to 160km/h in 3.5 seconds and reach a top speed of 340km/h.

F1 cars race over complex tracks with different types of turn and in changing race conditions, such as when it suddenly starts raining. Drivers, who may make more than 4,000 gear changes in a single race, need lightning fast reactions. They also have to be physically strong, so they can handle the huge gravitational forces on their bodies during sudden changes of speed and sharp turns.

WOW!

In his first nine F1 races, Lewis finished in a top three podium place every time!

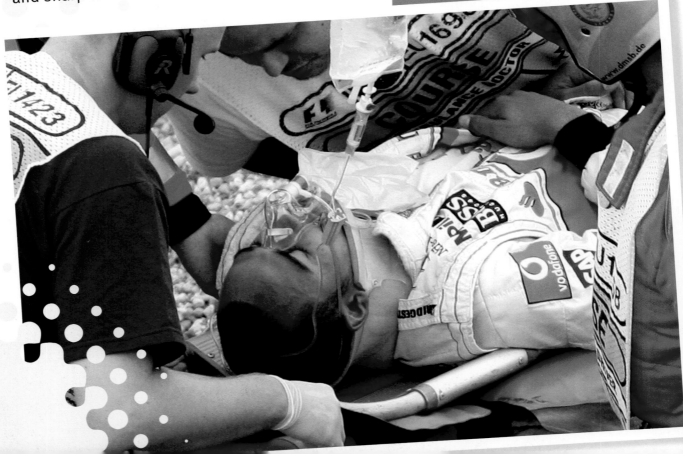

Lewis is stretchered off the track after a crash during qualifying for the 2007 European Grand Prix. He was able to take part in the race and finished ninth.

Lewis had always worked hard but now he faced the ultimate challenge and worked even harder. He had six months before the start of the 2007 F1 season to hone his skills. He worked tirelessly at McLaren every single day from eight in the morning to six at night, getting to know the team, the car, all the technology and the tactics involved. He would take technical manuals home to study before going to bed at 8pm to be fresh for the next intense day.

Finally, the week of Lewis' first F1 race arrived, at Albert Park in Australia. The week began with practice, then qualifying sessions to determine each car's position on the starting grid. Lewis qualified fourth for the race and went on to finish third, the first time in over 10 years a driver had finished in the top three in his **debut** F1 race.

Lewis takes the lead at the start of the Hungarian Grand Prix in 2007. Former F1 world champions like Damon Hill and Niki Lauda were astonished at how quickly Lewis took to Formula One racing.

Lewis followed up his debut with a string of impressive drives and finishes but all without a win. Victory came in his sixth race, the Canadian Grand Prix, which was also the first for which he had qualified in first place, known as **pole position**. Lewis went on to achieve five further pole positions out of 17 races. He nearly won the entire championship but a gearbox problem in the last race of the season meant that he finished seventh in the race and joint second in the overall championship.

INSPIRATION

Lewis dedicated his first ever Formula One race win to his father and said, "You wouldn't believe the amount of work he's put into my career."

Racing rivalries

Lewis had to overcome many issues during his first seasons in Formula One. These included rivalries with other drivers as well as other people's doubts about his abilities and lack of experience.

Lewis worked hard to win over his team's engineers and other staff with his dedication and desire to learn. He made an effort to visit every department of the McLaren team's headquarters regularly. The friendships he made there would help him in the races and seasons ahead.

Lewis was friends with fellow F1 drivers Robert Kubica from karting and Adrian Sutil with whom he had raced in Formula Three. But Lewis' aggressive driving style upset some more experienced drivers, rattled at his startling progress. None more so than his McLaren team-mate in 2007, Fernando Alonso.

TOP TIP

"If someone writes, or says, something about you…if it is positive, it is all good energy, and if it is negative you block it out." Lewis Hamilton

Lewis and Fernando Alonso look tense as they sit beside each other during the 2007 Brazilian Grand Prix.

Tensions between the two drivers in a Formula One team can run high. Each wants to outdo the other, yet both also have to work as part of a team. Fernando Alonso was the 2005 and 2006 World Champion. When he joined the McLaren team and was paid around £20 million a year (compared to Lewis's reported salary of £400,000), he expected to be treated like a champion.

Lewis respected Alonso, but competing against him was part of his job and he outperformed his team-mate in the early races. This led to angry scenes between the drivers and team boss, Ron Dennis. Despite being a **rookie**, Lewis managed to be strong and keep his focus on his driving. He matched Alonso point for point over the entire season ending on 109 points, one behind the world champion, Kimi Räikkönen.

INSPIRATION

"Lewis turned himself into the driver he is today. He did all the hard work. We just provided the support and the structure in which he could hone his skills. From day one Lewis impressed us with his level of commitment." – Martin Whitmarsh, CEO of Vodafone McLaren Mercedes.

Lewis and his team-mate for 2010, Jenson Button, joke around after coming first and second in the 2010 Canadian Grand Prix. The pair get on well even though they are competitive on the track.

A day in the life of Lewis Hamilton

Being an F1 driver is an intense job with many demands on Lewis's time. These include spending long hours at the team's headquarters or testing bases to help develop each season's new car. During the racing season (March to November) Lewis works hard with his team's engineers and other staff to make sure that his car is perfectly prepared for each race.

WOW!

With races held all over the world, a Formula One team may travel over 160,000km in a single season.

Lewis talks with his team engineers during preparations for the 2009 Spanish Grand Prix.

Lewis needs to be exceptionally fit. His neck, arms and upper body must be strong enough to withstand the massive **g-forces** that strain his body when he is racing at high speed. He also needs great stamina and fitness to drive at full tilt in testing, practice sessions, qualifying and then the race itself. In a Grand Prix race which lasts 90 minutes, Lewis will drive around 305km. He has to be totally focused for every single second of the race.

In the winter months when there are no races, Lewis trains between four and six hours a day and eats a healthy diet. He works out in the gym, often with fitness instructors and personal trainers with whom he also takes long cycle rides and walks. He likes to vary his training with some swimming and skiing too. Even in race season, he may do a couple of hours of fitness training on most days to stay in peak condition.

Lewis frequently listens to music (mainly rap and R&B) when he's travelling. At each destination, there are usually **sponsors** that Lewis must meet as well as appearances in front of the media and at other events. Lewis knows this is all part of his job and tries to be polite and helpful at all times. When Lewis does get some downtime, he likes to spend it with his family, playing his guitar, watching films or reading.

INSPIRATION

In an interview Lewis said: "I prefer to read more factual books, probably to learn something about an animal for example. It is great to have knowledge. The more knowledge, the more power!"

Vodafone Beach Kayak Challeng

Lewis crosses the finish line on the beach to win a kayaking race before the 2008 Australian Grand Prix. The race was part of a promotion for some of his team's sponsors.

The ups and downs of being a celebrity

After becoming Formula One World Champion, Lewis became a major celebrity. This has led to many great opportunities but has also had its disadvantages.

Lewis's celebrity allows him to raise a lot of money for charity, with fundraising appearances and, in 2007, by auctioning off one of his karts on the internet for £42,100. In 2008, he founded his own charity, the Lewis Hamilton Foundation, to raise money to improve the lives of children in the UK and abroad.

Lewis's fame has given him the opportunity to meet other celebrities, such as Beyoncé Knowles, Pharrell Williams and P. Diddy. In 2007, Lewis was invited to the MTV Awards in Las Vegas where he first met Nicole Scherzinger, lead singer of the Pussycat Dolls. The pair later became a couple even though constant travel for their individual careers keeps them apart much of the time.

INSPIRATION

Lewis remembered how friendly and polite F1 driver David Coulthard was when he met him as a boy. He has tried to act in the same way to sponsors and any young motor racing fans he meets.

Lewis stands with his girlfriend Nicole (centre), and Beyoncé Knowles before the 2009 Singapore Grand Prix.

The celebrity life also has its downside. Reporters and photographers follow Lewis' every move and at times he has found the amount of media interest unwelcome. In October 2007, he decided to live in Switzerland to escape some of the media attention, a move for which he was criticised in Britain. Further criticism followed two traffic offences, the first a speeding fine he received in France in 2007 and the second for deliberately spinning his wheels to create smoke in Australia in 2010.

A few weeks before the Australia incident, Lewis had asked his father to step down as his manager. He wanted a dedicated business manager so that he could have a more normal father and son relationship and told *Autosport* magazine, "What I am really, really excited about now is having my dad just as my dad."

WOW!

In 2009, a waxwork of Lewis was unveiled at Madame Tussauds in London alongside some of the world's most famous celebrities. Lewis had to sit still while 300 measurements of his body were made. The figure took six months to create and cost £150,000.

Attending press conferences and photo sessions like this one is part of Lewis' job but he finds it hard to deal with the media attention aimed at his private life.

The impact of Lewis Hamilton

In just four seasons in Formula One, Lewis Hamilton has already become one of the most famous names in motor racing. His exciting racing style has attracted large numbers of fans and he is a multi-millionaire with an estimated fortune of over £40 million. Lewis has announced his intention to spend the rest of his racing career at McLaren. Many F1 experts expect him to win more World Championships in the near future.

INSPIRATION

"At school you learn a lot about British history but I thought it was important for my life to learn about my background, about black history. I started to read about it – Muhammad Ali and Nelson Mandela. These are the figures I started to look up to and be inspired by." – Lewis Hamilton.

Lewis Hamilton receives his Member of the British Empire (MBE) medal from Queen Elizabeth II at Buckingham Palace in 2009. At 24, he was one of the youngest ever recipients of the award.

Lewis's impact, though, extends well beyond his sheer speed and skill on the track. He is the first black driver in Formula One and the first non-white driver to win races and championships in the sport's 60 year history. This makes him an important **role model** for other young black people looking to excel not just in motorsports but in many other fields.

In a newspaper interview in 2007, Lewis said, "It's good if I have attracted different people to F1. When I go to a petrol station and black and Asian kids come up and say, 'You're doing a great job' — it's a cool thing. All of a sudden they are watching F1 and they've got a reason to watch it. They can see I've got there. They see that if you approach something with the right mentality anything is possible. It doesn't have to be in F1 or racing."

In a sport which requires huge finance to compete, most drivers come from wealthy families. Lewis's far from wealthy start to life and his tale of determination, hard work and close family support is an inspiration for all young people.

TOP TIP

In an interview for Black History Month, Lewis was asked what handy words he would give to young people whatever their chosen career. He responded: "To stay focused and not give up. It is amazing what you can achieve if you keep plugging away. And it is really worth paying attention to people who have done it before you."

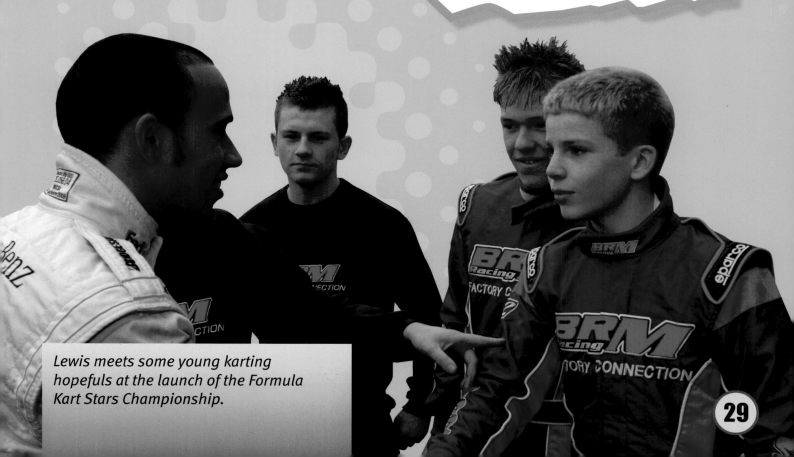

Lewis meets some young karting hopefuls at the launch of the Formula Kart Stars Championship.

Have you got what it takes to be a motor racing champion?

1) Are you fit and good at sports such as tennis, football, cricket and martial arts which require quick reactions?
a) Yes, I play lots of sports and love being in the middle of the action.
b) I could be fitter but I prefer more gentle sports such as snooker, walking or fishing.
c) No, I prefer watching sport to playing it.

2) How well do you do when you're playing computer racing games and simulations?
a) I almost always win and often get the highest score.
b) I do okay but only win now and then.
c) I'm always crashing or last!

3) Are you very competitive when you play sports or games?
a) I hate losing and try to improve so that I don't lose the next time.
b) No one likes losing but I don't give it much thought.
c) It doesn't really bother me.

4) Are you fascinated by machines and how they work?
a) Yes, I find everything about machines, especially cars and motorbikes, really interesting.
b) A little I guess, but mostly I just like how the cars look, not how the engines work.
c) I don't have to be, that's the mechanics' job isn't it?

5) Are you good at concentrating on things for long periods of time?
a) Yes, I can be very single-minded and focused on a single job.
b) Sometimes, but my mind does tend to wander a bit.
c) Not really, I get bored easily.

6) Are you prepared to sacrifice your social life to train long, long hours?
a) Yes, that would not bother me.
b) I'm happy to do some training but still want plenty of leisure time.
c) No way, José! Going out with my friends is what matters most to me.

RESULTS

Mostly As: It sounds like you may be cut out for motor racing. Why not try out karting or another motorsport like motocross on motorbikes and see if you catch the bug like Lewis.

Mostly Bs: You sound able to train and improve at a sport or pastime, but perhaps motor racing's not for you at the moment. Maybe it will interest you in the future, especially if you find out more about it.

Mostly Cs: It doesn't sound like the high speed thrills and commitment of motorsports is for you, well not yet, anyway.

Glossary

autobiography A book about a person's life written by that person.

debut A first appearance or performance in public.

emigrate To leave one country to settle, work and live in another country.

FIA Short for the Federation Internationale de l'Automobile, the organization which runs many major motor racing competitions.

g-force The force of gravity (g) on a body as it accelerates, such as is experienced by a space pilot during take-off or a racing driver during a Grand Prix race.

GP2 A motor racing competition one level below Formula One.

grid The arrangement of racing cars on the track showing their starting positions before a race.

mentor A trusted person who guides and advises another.

NASCAR A type of stock car race mostly held on oval tracks in North America.

pit lane The road at a racetrack which runs from the edge of the track to the team's garages.

podium A platform on which the first three drivers in a race stand to receive their trophies.

pole position The best position on the front of a starting grid given to the car or bike that qualifies with the fastest time.

qualifying Timed laps before a motor race with the fastest drivers starting at the front.

role model A successful person in sport or some other field. The way they behave is often copied by others, especially young people.

rookie A driver making his debut season in a competition.

safety car A vehicle which comes onto the track to limit racing cars' speeds as all cars have to stay behind it.

sponsors Companies or very wealthy individuals who provide equipment or money to a driver or race team.

valet Someone who cleans motor vehicles, often those for sale in a garage or motor showroom.

Index

INSPIRATIONAL LIVES

Contents of new titles in the series

Kelly Holmes
978 0 7502 6480 8

Golden girl
A difficult beginning
Early promise
Joining the Army
Back on track
Injury strikes
Despair turns to joy
Highs and lows
Olympic glory
A nation celebrates
Life after running
A day in the life of Kelly Holmes
The impact of Kelly Holmes
Have you got what it takes to be
  an Olympic champion?

Tony Hawk
978 0 7502 6483 9

"The best day of my life"
A hyperactive child
Bitten by the boarding bug
Getting good
Turning pro
High school star
Building Birdhouse
Ups and downs
Video game star
Business booms
Giving something back
A day in the life of Tony Hawk
The impact of Tony Hawk
Have you got what it takes to be
  a pro skateboarder?

Lewis Hamilton
978 0 7502 6481 5

World Champion!
Growing up
Starting karting
Moving home
Making sacrifices
Joining McLaren
Success and setbacks
Life in GP2
Welcome to F1
Racing rivalries
A day in the life of Lewis Hamilton
The ups and downs of being
  a celebrity
The impact of Lewis Hamilton
Have you got what it takes to be
  a motor racing champion?

Usain Bolt
978 0 7502 6482 2

The world's fastest human
A lively child
Success comes early
Reality check
Time to rebuild
The world takes notice
Olympic superstar
Return of a hero
Lightning strikes twice
Awards and injuries
A day in the life of Usain Bolt
An inspiration to others
The impact of Usain Bolt
Have you got what it takes to be
  a record-breaking athlete?

WAYLAND